Grandma's New Home

Presented by

Treasure's Journey

Dedication

"Keep dreaming because one day your dreams will come true."

The Dreamer

Today is Friday and on Friday's momma picks me up early from school and we go visit grandma for the weekend. We take the train because she lives two hours away. Although momma has a car, we like riding the train instead of driving.

We have so much fun riding on the train. Momma and I play games, listen to music and she lets me bring one of my favorite toys on the train.

We visit grandma a lot because she is very sick, and momma said she will be moving to her new home soon.

A nurse comes to help grandma get everything that she needs because she is unable to do a lot on her own.

Whenever I ask momma what grandma will do in her new home, she always says, "Whatever she wants because she will feel all better." That always makes me feel better.

When we go to grandma's house, I get to see my cousin Aiden and we have a lot of fun together.

This time Aiden is coming back to live with us because his mom and dad are in the Army. I am excited that he will be living with us. Daddy already fixed up the guest room for him to use.

When we got off the train, we took an uber to grandma's house and Aiden met us at the door.

When I walked in the house, I ran to grandma as she opened her arms to hug me and said, "How's my favorite girl?" I love lying in her arms. She always smells like warm vanilla

After sitting with my grandma, Aiden and I went to play outside with some of our other friends.

After all our friends went in the house, Aiden and I sat on grandma's porch eating red jellybeans.

We love eating the red jellybeans because it makes our teeth and tongues red.

We ate lots and lots of jelly beans; after we ate Jelly beans we rode our bikes down the hill near grandma's house.

We had grandma's favorite meal for dinner which was corn bread, black eye peas and fried chicken. She did not have much of an appetite so she just went to bed early.

Aiden and I stayed up all night watching cartoons and eating snacks. Momma let us stay up past our bed time since we did not have to go to school in the morning.

On Sunday morning, Aiden and I helped momma cook breakfast. We made pancakes, sausage and eggs. Grandma did not eat much for breakfast either. Her nurse ate breakfast with us because grandma was very tired and just slept a lot.

After lunch it was time for us to go home. We gave grandma a kiss and took an uber to the train station. During the train ride momma was very sad. I asked momma if she was ok and she said, "Yes sweet heart, I am ok".

When we got home I showed Aiden his room and helped him put all his things away. Aiden was so excited because he never had his own bedroom before. Aiden did not have a lot of things so momma and daddy brought him things to put in his new room.

Aiden and I woke up early the next day for school because he wanted to get to school early to meet his new teacher.

After school momma and daddy picked us up. When we got in the car, momma said "Remember when I said that grandma was preparing to move to her new home?" Aiden and I said yes we remember. Momma said that grandma moved to her new home late last night.

Aiden and I began to feel sad but momma said, "It's ok to be sad sometimes, it is hard to understand when someone you love leaves because you will miss them a lot, but we can always talk about them and all the fun things we remember. That way we will always keep our love ones alive in our hearts."

Aiden looked up and smiled and said, "I have many fun memories of grandma".

On the way home daddy stopped to get ice cream because he said we could all use a treat. Aiden and I were very excited because we both love ice cream.

After we got our ice cream we sat on the bench and shared all of our happy memories of grandma. It made us all feel better about her moving to her new home in heaven.

Although she is in a new home far away, we keep her close to us by keeping her in our hearts.

We will always remember all of the fun we had with grandma.

Made in the USA
Columbia, SC
08 May 2024

35366244R00015